The Mayhew Manor of Tisbury

THE MAYHEW MANOR
OF TISBURY

ADDRESS PREPARED FOR
THE NEW YORK BRANCH

OF

THE ORDER OF COLONIAL LORDS OF MANORS IN AMERICA

BY

IDA M. WIGHTMAN

UNDER THE SUPERVISION OF

COLONEL CHARLES EDWARD BANKS

Author of the History of Martha's Vineyard, &c.

BALTIMORE
1921

WILLIAM ALEXANDER, EARL OF STERLING FROM WHOM THOMAS MAYHEW
MADE HIS FIRST PURCHASE. BORN 1557. DIED 1641.

THE MAYHEW MANOR OF TISBURY*

It is a fact unknown in history, except perhaps to a few local antiquarians, that the island of Martha's Vineyard, located just south of Cape Cod and now a part of the Commonwealth of Massachusetts, was at one time under the jurisdiction of the Province of New York, and constituted one of its first three county governments. Martha's Vineyard, together with the Elizabeth Islands, Nantucket, and No Man's Land, was incorporated November 1, 1683, by the Provincial Assembly of New York, as Duke's County, coincident with the creation of King's County (now Brooklyn), and Queen's County (Long Island), but for twenty years before that date it had been an integral part of the Province of New York.

In order to understand the political relationship of these far-flung isles of the southeastern New England coast to the New York government, it is necessary to hark back to the early settlement of this country when King James established the Council for New England, which gave this territory to certain of the nobility, and other prominent Englishmen interested in the colonization of the New World. This Council for New England had regulated the affairs of this territory as best it could by long distance orders in Council granting Patent rights to enterprising Englishmen who were ready to exploit its unknown riches for the glorification of the Crown of England, and incidentally, for their own profit. For thirty years this corporate body had been in active operation until, in 1635, it found that the maximum of its powers and usefulness had been reached and in their wisdom the remaining active members deemed it wise to divide the territory among themselves as best they could, with their limited knowledge of the geography and nomenclature of it, and surrender their Charter to the Crown.

This division, which was effected on February 3, 1634-5, and confirmed three years later, is of especial interest to this study because two of the active members, Sir Ferdinando Gorges, and William Alexander, Earl of Stirling, "drew" certain

* The following are also the various ways of spelling this name. viz.: Tissebury, Tisselbury, Tysbery, Tissbury and Tisburie. (Vol. II, page 16 of the *Annals of West Tisbury, History of Martha's Vineyard*, by Charles Edward Banks.)

5

islands on the southeastern coast of New England, as their shares in this territorial lottery, and these later resulted in conflicting claims.

Sir Ferdinando Gorges was the Lord Proprietor of the Province of Maine, and in addition was awarded that region from the Piscataqua to the Sagadahoc as specified in the records of the division by the Council;[1] "and hereunto is to be added the North halfe of the Isles of Shoals & also the Isles of Capawock, Nautican &c near unto Cape Codd." Lord Stirling was granted certain territory adjacent to that of Gorges in Maine, and, as decreed by the Council,[2] "hereunto is to belong the Island called Mattawack or the Long Island."

Four years later, on April 3rd, 1639, King Charles granted a charter to Sir Ferdinando Gorges conferring extraordinary prerogatives in government of this territory in Maine, and by its terms "the Isles of Capawock and Nautican, near unto Cape Cod" were specifically included. This charter, therefore, gave to Gorges undoubted sovereign rights over Martha's Vineyard which was then erroneously called by the Indian name of Capawock, a name properly belonging only to a small portion of the island.

Neither Lord Stirling nor Sir Ferdinando Gorges had come in person to this new world to learn by personal observation the extent of the territory comprised in their Patents, though both were represented here by agents; the former by Mr. James Forrett, and the latter by Mr. Richard Vines who held the title of Steward-General of the Province of Maine, he having been one of the pioneer settlers of that Province.

Forrett doubtless resided in New Amsterdam, probably because of its proximity to Long Island, the most valuable part of Lord Stirling's property, and from his activities it appears that he was not modest in his claims of proprietorship on behalf of the Earl of Stirling; Martha's Vineyard, Nantucket and the adjacent islands being claimed by him to be a part of his master's holdings. It is not known upon what ground he based this claim, but that he maintained it to the profit of his master is a matter of record.

In September, 1641, Forrett journeyed to Boston to complain to Governor Winthrop about the unwarranted entry of some people from Lynn, Massachusetts, upon the lands of Lord Stirling on Long Island. Incidentally he went there to

Banks History of Martha's Vineyard, I, 73.
Records of Colonial New England, 69, 70, 83.

encourage lawful immigration under proper acknowledgment of proprietary rights, and this he succeeded in accomplishing. He met while there, possibly by chance, Mr. Thomas Mayhew, an early resident of Watertown, who was then deep in the maelstrom of financial trouble, and it is presumed laid before him the desirability of retrieving his fortunes in a new, unsettled region. The advantages of the virgin islands of Nantucket and Martha's Vineyard which Forrett claimed as part of his master's domain, were doubtless represented in glowing terms by this early prototype of our modern promoter. Whether Mayhew had ever seen these islands may be doubted, but in despair of mind because it had "pleased God to frown upon him in his outward estate," he accepted this opportunity of beginning a new career under different conditions, and restoring his vanishing fortunes.

Such may well have been the process by which Mayhew's attention was directed to these fertile islands of the sea, which, as Underhill had noted several years before, were "as yet uninhabited," and Mayhew, then in his fiftieth year, determined to purchase them and start a new home, and possibly erect a new colony, for these islands were situated without the chartered bounds of the territory of the Company of Massachusetts Bay.

"Meanwhile, however, an unexpected development occurred. 'Mr. Richard Vynes,' wrote Mayhew, 'Steward Gen'll to Sir Ferdynando Gorges, heareing of it, Enterupted showing me his Master's Pattent and his Power, insomuch that I was convinced by him and Thomas Gorges who was then Governour of the Province of Maine that (it) was realy Sir Ferdynandoes Right.' It somewhat arouses our curiosity to know how Vines,—living a hundred miles distant, should have become aware within a few days of the sale by Forrett to Mayhew, unless we infer, as we are justified in doing by the light of subsequent events, that Mayhew was not satisfied with the title of Lord Stirling, and desiring to satisfy all possible claimants and secure deeds from each, asked Vines to come to Watertown to effect the transfer of his master's right. However, Mayhew says that Vines 'heareing of it, Enterupted,' which would indicate that the agent of Gorges acted independently upon learning of the action of Forrett, and Mayhew, in order to secure himself, as he says, 'for a some of Money did obtaine from said Vynes a Graunt alsoe.' Again he wrote on the same topic: 'Meeteing with Mr. Vynes steward general to Sir Ferdinando Gorges whom I then had much interest in he solemnely p'fesses it was his Masters so whereupon I had it graunted by him & did p'cede mostly uppon that graunt, Mr. Tho. Gorges then gov'nor (of the Province of Maine) approuveing of it.'"[5]

Accordingly Mayhew entered into an agreement with the agent of Stirling for the purchase of Nantucket, and on October 13, 1641, the deed of sale was executed by Forrett which granted to Thomas Mayhew, a Watertown merchant, and to Thomas Mayhew, Junior, his son, the right "to Plant and Inhabit upon Nantucket and two other small Islands adjacent," meaning Muskeget and Tuckernuck.

The price paid for this property, £40, is not stated in this document[4] which is given in full:

These presents doth witness that I, James Forrett, Gentleman, who was sent over into these Parts of America. By the honourable the Lord Sterling with a commission for the ordering and Disposing of all the Island that Lyeth Between Cape Cod hudsons river and hath better unto consimed his agency without any considerations. Do hereby Grant unto Thomas Mayhew of Watertown, merchant, and to Thomas Mayhew his son, free liberty and full power to them and their associates to Plant and Inhabit upon Nantuckett and two other small Islands adjacent, and to enjoy the said Islands to them and their heirs & assigns forever. provided that the said Thomas Mayhew and Thomas Mayhew his son or either of them or their associates Do Render and Pay yearly unto the honourable the Lord Sterling, his heir or assigns such an acknowledgment as shall be thought fitt by John Winthrop Esq the elder or any two magistrates in Massachusetts Bay Being chosen for that end and purpose by the honourable the Lord Sterling or his Deputy and By the said Thomas Mayhew his son or associates; it is agreed that the government that the said Thomas Mayhew and Thomas Mayhew his son and their associates shall sett up shall Be such as is now established in the Massachusetts afore-said, and that the said Thomas Mayhew & Thomas Mayhew his son and their associates shall have as much privilege touching their planting Inhabiting and enjoying of all and every part of the Premises as By the patent is granted to the Patent of the Massachusetts aforesaid and their associates.

In witness hereof I the said James Forrett have hereunto sett my hand and seal this 13th day of October, 1641.

                                        JAMES FORRETT.

Signed Sealed and Delivered in the presence of
Robert
Nicholas Davison
Richard Stileman[5]

Banks, *History of Martha's Vineyard*, I, 73.
Edgartown Records, I, 12.
[5] Nicholas Davison was a Charlestown merchant, agent of Matthew Cradock, and later a land-owner on the Vineyard, but not a resident.
Richard Stileman was of Cambridge at this date, but later removed to Portsmouth. It is probable that this document was executed in Boston.

"This resulted, doubtless, in a conference between the conflicting interests, and as a consequence further amplification of Mayhew's territorial jurisdiction. Forrett added 'Martin's' Vineyard and the Elizabeth Islands, in a second instrument which he drew up, and authorized the grantees to plant upon and inhabit those parts"[7] and this document reads as follows:[8]

' Whereas By virtue of a commission from the Lord Sterling, James Forrett, Gentleman, hath granted Liberty and full Power unto Thomas Mayhew of Watertowh, merchant, and Thomas Mayhew his son, and their associates to Plant the Island of Nantucket according to the article In a deed to that purpose expressed: Now for as much as the said Island hath not Been yett whole surrendered whereby it may appear that Comfortable accomodations for themselves and their asscoiates will be found there, this therefore shall serve to testifye that I, the said James Forrett, by virtue of my said commission. Do hereby grant unto the said Thomas Mayhew and Thomas Mayhew his son and their associates, as much to plant upon Martins Vinyard and Elizabeth Isles as they have by virtue heretofore of the Deed granted unto them for Nantuckett as therein plainly In all considerations Both on the Right honourable the Lord Sterling's part and on the said Thomas Mayhew & Thomas Mayhew his son and their associates Doth appear In Witness whereof I, the said James Forrett have hereunto sett my hand the 23rd Day of October, Annoque Domini 1641.

JAMES FORRITT.

Signed and delivered In presence of us
                his
John   X   Vahane"
             mark
Garret Church[10]

"But this was not entirely satisfactory, and so he concluded to 'make assurance doubly sure' by securing the rights as well from the Gorges interests; and two days later the following instrument executed by Vines, authorized the elder Mayhew to 'plant and inhabit upon the Island Capawok alias Martins Vineyard,' "[11] as set forth in the following copy:[12]

"I, Richard Vines of Saco, Gentleman, Steward General for Sir Ferdinando Georges, Knight and Lord Proprietor of the Province of Maine and the Islands of Cappawok and Nautican, Do by these presents give full

[7] Banks, History of Martha's Vineyard, 1, 82, 83.

[8] Edgartown Records, I, 11.

[9] John Vahane (Vaughan) was a resident of Watertown in 1633, and bore a not very savory reputation for a number of years.

[10] Garret Church was also of Watertown. From the appearance of these two names, it is presumed the document was signed in Mayhew's home town.

[11] Banks, History of Martha's Vineyard, I, 83.

[12] Edgartown Records, I, 9.

power and authority unto Thomas Mayhew, Gentleman, his agents and associates to plant and Inhabit upon the Islands Capawok alias Martins Vinyard with all privileges and Rights thereunto belonging to enjoy the premises to himself heirs and associates forever, yielding and Paying unto the said Ferdinando Gorges, his heirs and assigns annually, or two Gentlemen Independently By each of them chosen Shall Judge to Be meet by way of acknowledgement.

Given under my hand this 25th Day of October, 1641.

RICHARD VINES.

Witness:
Thomas Payne[13]
Robert Long[14]

Thus doubly assured of his title to the islands from two rival claimants to them, the elder Mayhew, not wishing to invite further complications, proceeded to satisfy one more possible proprietor—the aboriginal squatters—and shortly

Navis ex arboris trunco igne excavata

"OUR EARLIEST FERRY"

Representation of Indians crossing the Vineyard Sound in a Canoe made by burning out a trunk of a tree.

after procured from the Indians their "rights" to his newly acquired domain. Actual possession of the islands was accomplished the year following. Upon this, the Rev. Experience Mayhew, grandson of the elder Thomas, has written as follows: "In 1642 he (Thomas Mayhew) sends Mr. Thomas Mayhew Junior his only Son, being then a young scholar, about 21 years of Age, with some other Persons to the Vineyard, where they settled at the East End, and quickly after the Father followed."

Having thus detailed the acquisition of Martha's Vineyard by the ancestral manorial family of Mayhew's, it will next be

[13] There was a Thomas Paine, resident of Salem, another resident of Dedham, and a third of Yarmouth. It is not possible to identify this witness. It was not Mayhew's step-son as he was only nine years old.
[14] Robert Long was resident of Charlestown.

of interest to learn the origin and descent of the Lords of Tisbury Manor.[15]

"The name of Mayhew and the Vineyard are almost synonymous, and it will be interesting as well as instructive to learn something of the family which exercised such a sway over the early destinies of our island. The origin of the name is explained satisfactorily by a learned historical scholar of England, himself a descendant, and the following extracts are made from his account:

"As an English family name it is most frequently met with in the South and West of this island, and few parish registers in the Counties of Hereford, Gloucester, Wilts and Dorset can be opened without presenting us with examples. It is spelt in many ways, varying from the extended form of Mayhowe to that of Mao, and often, as it will frequently appear, clipped down and reduced to May to the loss of its concluding syllable.[16] One lesson is taught by the diversity and variety, viz:—the identity of Mayhew and Mayo, and from this consideration a ray of light is thrown upon the derivation of the name. An early occurrence of the name, and in its extended form, is found in Glover's Roll of Arms, supposed by Sir Harris Nicholas to date from between 1245 and 1250. Herbert le Fitz Mayhewe is there mentioned as bearing 'party d'azur & de goulz one trois leonseaux rampant d'or,' and Woodward in his History of Wales, page 415, narrates that account to the old copy of S. Davids Annals. The Welsh slew Sir Herbert Fitz-Mahu apparently in 1246, near the castle of Morgan Cam. The same Roll of Arms gives the clue to the origin of the name as a Christian name; in the case of Mahewe de Lovayne, Mayhew de Columbers and Maheu de Redmain. There can be little doubt that it is here a softened form of Matthew. Bardsley in his ' English Surnames" mentioned two other instances, Adam fil. Maheu, and Mayhew de Basingbourne, from the Parliamentary Writs. Lower, (Patronymica Brittannica, 219, 221), takes the same view."

Shakespeare in King Lear, Act III, scene 4 says:

"The Prince of Darkness is a Gentleman
Modo he's called and Mahu."

"The family has its principal habitats in Cornwall, at Lostwithiel, Looe, Bray and Morval, to which belonged John Mayow, Fellow of All Souls, Oxford, and that Mayow of Clevyan, in St. Columb Major, who was hanged on a tavern

[15] Banks, *History of Martha's Vineyard*, I, 104.

[16] As an example of the loss of the final syllable, the following may be noted: Walter Mayo vel Meye admissus in Artibus 26 June 1511, (Gough Mss. 7, Bod. Lib.); the will of Robert Mayo of Broughton Gifford 16 Nov. 1572, in the Perogative Court, though his family name was usually written May, as in the Wiltshire visitations; the will of Henry Mayo alias May, of Kellways, Wilts, 1661.

11

sign-post as a rebel against the injunctions of Edward VI,
concerning religion. Dorsetshire has one family in the Visitation; Gloucestershire, at Kempley, Tetbury, Charfield;
Herefordshire, at Tottenham; Northamptonshire, at Holmden,
in the Visitation of 1619; Norfolk, at Billockby and Clippesby;
Suffolk at Clopton, Helmington and Bedingfield, and in Wiltshire more than one family of the name are found including
Mayhew of Dinton in the Visitations of 1565 and 1623, whose
pedigree is inserted in this article.[17]

"Of noted persons of the name is Richard Mayo, otherwise
Mayeo, Maiewe, Mayhue, etc., who was born near Hungerford,
educated at Winchester, became a fellow of the New College
in 1459; after passing through the lower orders he became
Chancellor of Oxford, 1503, and Bishop of Hereford in 1504.
He died in April, 1516.[18]

In the Records of the Commissioners for the United Colonies,
there appeared a letter, now in the Connecticut Archives,[19]
written by Governor Mayhew, sealed with arms which, upon
examination, proved to be the arms, with a mullet for difference, of the Mayhew family of Dinton, Wiltshire, a county
family of considerable distinction.[20]

The pedigree of this family follows, with an illustration of
the Church of St. John the Baptist, where Thomas Mayhew
was baptized, April 1, 1593.

"These facts, taken in connection with the bestowal by
Mayhew of the names of Tisbury and Chilmark on two adjoining towns on Martha's Vineyard, (the latter settlement having
been originally chartered as Tisbury Manor,, and the fact
that Tisbury and Chilmark are adjoining parishes in Wiltshire,
and separated by a few miles only from Dinton, made it quite
evident that this locality was the one which should reveal his
family connection.

"In April, 1898, the author,[21] during a visit to England, was
guest by previous appointment with the Vicar of Tisbury,
the Rev. F. E. Hutchinson, who is of the same stock as our
family of the New England Hutchinsons. He spent two days
at the vicarage and had ample time to make a thorough exami-

---

[17] Banks. *History of Martha's Vineyard*, I, 104, 105.
[18] *Genealogical Account of the Mayo and Eaton Families*, by Rev. Canon
Mayo, vicar of Long Burton, Dorset. London, 1882.
[19] *Conn. Col. Records 1678-1689*, pp. 504-506.
[20] Banks. *History of Martha's Vineyard*, I, 105-106.
[21] Chas. E. Banks, Senior Surgeon, U. S. P. H. S.

12

PEDIGREE OF MAYHEW OF DINTON

Harl. Mss. 1181, 1443.
Herald's Visitations, 1565, 1623.
Hoare, Wiltshire, IV, 102; V, 66.

Arms: Argent, on a chevron between three sea mews, sa. five lozenges of the field, with a crescent for difference (1565).

Simon Mayow =
Gent.,
of Dynton,
com. Wilts.

Robert Mayow = Joan Bridmore
eldest sonne and ¦ dau. of John of Tisbury,
heire of Dynton, ¦   co. Wilts.
com. Wilts.

Joan Hamon = John Mayow = Joan Prest
dau. of Ralph ¦ of Dynton ¦ She mar. 2d
of Everash in ¦ bur. 25 Feb., ¦ Robert
co. Somerset. ¦ 1563. Will ¦ Bownde, 4
          ¦ 20 Sept., ¦ Sept.,
          ¦ 1562. ¦ 1564.

(1)   (2)

Edward   Thomas   Henry   Walter   Two Daughters.
2d son   3d son.   of   of
Fonthill   Dynton.   Chilmark.
Wilts.
=   =   =
Agnes | King   Elizabeth   AliceCote
                           bur. 6   of
                           April,   Chilmark.
                           1577.

Henry   Ralph   Richard   William   Maud   Cuthbert   Robert   John   Dennis   Two   Matthew   Edward   Joan
(eldest).   bur. 1561. bur. 1558. Alice   (eldest).   four   daus.   of   1571.   Cicely
                          Jane   daus.   Tisbury.   Jane   Anne
                                                                                            1574.   Alice
                                                                                            Elizabeth William
                                                                                            1577.

Ralph   Cuthbert   Mary   Thomas
                                            Dorothy   bp. 1593.

Ralph

CHURCH OF S. JOHN THE BAPTIST WHERE THOMAS MAYHEW WAS BAPTISED APRIL 1ST, 1593

14

STONE FONT. CHURCH OF S. JOHN THE BAPTIST. USED AT THE BAPTISM OF
THOMAS MAYHEW THE ELDER

*(A replica of this font, in English Oak, was presented by the family of the author to Grace
Church, Vineyard Haven, in memory of a deceased relative, several
years ago, and may be seen in that church)*

nation of the old parish registers of Tisbury, which are extant
from the year 1563, including the original and a parchment
copy of almost contemporary date. Below extracts from the
parish register are given, which include all of the name of
Mayhew in its several variations, as well as some relating to
persons connected with the family by marriage mentioned in
wills, to be hereafter given, during the period necessary for
our purpose.[22]

EXTRACTS FROM THE PARISH REGISTER OF TISBURY, Co. WILTS.

BAPTISMS

1583	Sept. 13, Henry, son of. . . . . .Maoh
1589	May 1, Elizabeth, daughter of Matthew Maho.
1591	Jan'y 17, John, son of Matthew Mayoo.
1593	April 1, THOMAS, SON of MATHEW MAHO.
1595 6	Feb. 8, Jone, daughter of Mathew Mayhoe.
1598	Dec. 18, Alice, daughter of Mathew Maiho.
1599	
1600	Mar. 15, Katherine, daughter of Mathew Maio.
1602	April 14 Edward, son of Mathew Mayhow.

MARRIAGES.

1573	Nov. 24, Myhell May and Jone Vanner.
1575	April 21, Thomas Maow? and Alyce Waterman?)
1578	Nov. 23, An Maio and Thomas Turner.
1579	Aug. 3, An Maio and John Waterman.
1587	Octo. 2, MATHEW MAOW and ALES BARTER.

BURIALS.

1586	July 14, Ales wyffe of Thomas Maow.
1590	June 1, Thomas Maow

Reproduction of entry in Parish Register showing record of baptism
of Thomas Mayhew.

"The marriage above indicated by capitals is that of the
parents of Gov. Thomas Mayhew, and his baptism is likewise
printed in the same type. Attention need scarcely be drawn
to the various ways the name is entered in the register. In
the[22] baptisms given, eight in all, there are seven different
spellings. This entry of the baptism of Thomas, son of Mathew
Maho, April 1st, 1593, probably within a few days of his birth,
is not absolutely conclusive evidence of identity with our
Thomas, but taken in connection with the facts relating to
the reappearance on Martha's Vineyard of the names of Tisbury
Manor (which is situated in the parish of Tisbury, England,)
and Chilmark the adjoining hamlet, and the name of Matthew,
which for succeeding generations appeared in the Martha's
Vineyard family, it becomes one of those cases where an affirmative conclusion is clearly inferential.

[22] Banks: History of Martha' Vineyard. I. 105 108.

16

"Corroborative evidence is also available in respect to Governor Mayhew's age, which corresponds approximately with the record of this baptism. The double dating of that period from January 1 to March 25, enters the problem to give it some slight complications, but as he was born near the dividing line between the new and the old years 1592 and 1593, his several statements regarding the great number of years he attained (evidently a source of pride to him) lead us readily to conclude that with the proneness which he exhibited to reiterate his longevity, he unintentionally adopted 1592 as his birth year, when it was in reality 1593, and that a further source of error lies in the confusion which may result from such general statements as that he was eighty-seven years of age, or in his 87th yeare half out. The following are all the references regarding his age which have been thus far observed, and it will be noticed that the first one, before he had grown to riper years and indulged the pardonable satisfaction at attaining great age, is the only correct one as compared to the date of baptism. It bears out the theory that he unconsciously overstated his age as he grew older.

"1. On Sept. 15, 1664, he wrote, 'I am 71 and 5 monthes at present.'[23] This would carry his birth back to about 2-15-1593. (Within one month prior to April 15, 1593, which agrees with the baptism.)

"2. On 24 (6), 1678, he wrote, 'It hath pleased God to keepe me alyve and verry well, to write thus much in my 87th yeare hallf out.'[24] This would carry his birth back to about 12-24-1591. (Feb. 24, 1591-2.)

"3. In his will dated June 16, 1681, he began: "I, Thomas Mayhew of Edgartown upon the Vineyard in this ninetieth year of my age,' This would carry his birth back to some time between June 17, 1591, and June 16, 1592."[25]

"4. On April 13, 1682, Matthew Mayhew, his grandson, announced to Gov. Thomas Hickley of Plymouth the death of his grandfather as follows: "It pleased God of his great goodness as to continue my honoured grandfather's life to a great age (wanting but six days of ninety years), so to give the comfort of his life, and to ours as well as his comfort in his sickness (which was six days).'[26]

[23] *Mass. Hist. Coll.*, 4th series, vol. 7, p. 40.
[24] *Plymouth Colony Records*, vol. 10, p. 406.
[25] Banks: *History of Martha's Vineyard*, 1, 108–109.
[26] *Mass. Hist. Coll.*, 4th series, vol. 5, p. 61.

"Previously to the author's visit to Tisbury a personal search of the Wiltshire wills deposited at Somerset House relating to the Archdeaconry of Sarum, in which the parishes of Tisbury, Chilmark and Dinton are situated, was made. There were found, among others of the family, the wills of Matthew Mayhew, the father of Thomas, and of Agnes Mayhew, an aunt of Thomas, in both of which documents his name occurs as a beneficiary. The full copy of the will of Matthew is here presented:"[27]

PRINCIPAL REGISTRY OF PROBATE (WILTSHIRE), ARCHDEACONRY OF SARUM, VIII, 224.

In the name of God Amen. I Mathew Maihew of Tisbury in the county of wilts yeoman being in good health and of perfect memory thankes bee to god for it doe make constitute and ordeine this my last will and testament in manner and form following First I bequeath my soule into the handes of Almighty God my maker and redeemer and my body to bee buried in the Church or Churchyard of Tisbury aforesaid. Itm I give and bequeath to the prish Church of Tisbury iiis vid. Itm I give and bequeath to the poore people of the aforesaid Tisbury iis iiiid. Itm I give and bequeath to my sonne Thomas Maihew Forty pounds of good and lawfull monie of England whereof twenty pounds to bee paid him by my Executor wthin one whole yeare after my decease and the other twenty pounds to bee paid by my Executor within five yeares after the payment of the first twenty pounds in manner and forme following, viz: fower pounds evy year until the sume of twenty pounds bee paid and the five yeares expired. Itm I give and bequeath unto my sonne Edward Maihew six and forty pounds of good and lawfull monie of England whereof six and twenty to bee paid him by my executor within one whole yeare after my decease and the other twenty pounds to bee paid unto him by my executor after the same manner and at the same times wch are prescribed for the payment of the last twenty pounds of my sonne Thomas his portion Itm I give and bequeath untonmy daughter Joane Maihewe six and forty pounds of good and lawfull monie of England whereof six and twenty pounds to bee paid within one whole yeare after my decease and the other twenty pounds to bee paid after the same manner and at the same times wch are prescribed for the last payment of my sonne Thomas his portion Itm I give and bequeath unto my daughter Alice Maihew six and forty pounds of good and lawfull monie of England to be paid unto her by my executor after such manner and at such times as my daughter Joane Maihewes portion is to be paid Itm I give and bequeath unto my daughter Katherine Maihew six and forty pounds to bee paid unto her by my executor after the same manner and at the same times wch are prscribed for the payment of my other two daughters portion All the rest of my goods and chattels moveable and unmovable I give and bequeath unto my sonne John Maihew whom I make my whole and sole executor of this my last will and testamt Itm I doe constitute and appoint John Bracher of Tisbury Edward Bracher of Tisbury Richard Langly of Boreham and John Gilbert of Deny Sutton ovrseers of this my last will and testament In witness

Banks: *History of Martha's Vineyard*, I, 109 110 111.

18

whereof I have hereunto subscribed my hande the last day of August in the year of our Lord 1612

The Marke of Mathewe Maihewe.

In the prnce of
> Luke Simpson
> John Gilbert
> John Turner
> John Bracher

Memorand. That if my sonne Thomas Maihewe Edward Maihewe Joane Maihewe Alice Maihewe Katherine Maihewe or any one of them doe chaunce to dye before they have receaved theire portions then my will is that the portions of the parties deceased shall equally bee divided amongst the rest then liveing

Witnesses hereunto
> Luke Simpson John Gilbert
> John Gilbert
> John Turner
> John Bracher

Proved 27th June 1614

"The will of Agnes Mayhew of Tisbury, dated Jan. 12, 1606, gives to 'Thomas the son of my brother Matthew, five pounds,' and it was proved June 24, 1612 (Arch. Sarum, VIII, 168).

"With respect to the connection of this Tisbury twig with the armorial family of Dinton, it is to be observed that Matthew described himself as 'yeoman,' which may not disqualify him as a cadet scion of the armigerous family, particularly in view of the fact that Governor Mayhew, his son, used a seal, which he must have obtained in England, cut with the arms of the Dinton family, and having as a mark of difference the mullet, indicating that he was descended from the third son of the armorial grantee.[28] The tabular pedigree which appears herewith, showing the Dinton family as given in the Harleian manuscripts and in Hoare's Wiltshire, to which have been added some facts obtained from wills and other original sources, fails to afford us any information concerning the descendants of Thomas, the third son of Robert Mayhew, and the author strongly suspects that it is to him, whose Christian name Governor Mayhew bore, we must look for an extension of the pedigree. The laws of primogeniture, which existed at that period, and which were so carefully observed by the heralds, afforded little consideration for cadet branches of county familes, and we are at present reduced to conjecture as to the relationship of Matthew to the Dinton stock, a conclusion

[28] Many years ago there was issued by the late Jonathan Mayhew of Buffalo. N. Y., a pictorial "family tree" which has, erroneously, depicted on it the coat armor of the Mayhews of Hemingston, Suffolk.

which seems reasonable to be made in the affirmative from all
the collateral facts. It is to be observed that the name of
Simon Mayhew, which appears at the head of the tabular
pedigree, was used by the Martha's Vineyard family as early as
1687, which may be classed as additional corroborative testi-
mony. Unfortunately the parish registers of Chilmark are
missing prior to 1653, and although Bishops' transcripts exist
in the Diocesan Registry at the Salisbury Cathedral, 'Our
Lady Church of Sarum,' they contain no Mayhew entires.[29]
A branch of the Dinton family, represented by Walter, the
fourth son of Robert of Dinton, lived in Chilmark, which is
the next parish to Tisbury and nearer Dinton. Walter Mayhew
'de Chilmark, gentleman' made his will Aug. 30, 1604, which
was proven Dec. 24, 1606, and in it he makes a bequest to the
poor of Fountell (Fonthill) where his elder brother Edward

SEAL USED BY GOVERNOR MAYHEW
From the Connecticut Archives.

resided.[30] No references to Tisbury or relatives outside of
his family appear (Arch. Sarum, Rotula XV)."

"John Mayhew of Dinton, however, the eldest son of that
generation, in his will dated Sept. 20, 1562, bequeaths a small
sum 'to the Church of Tisbury,' besides to his own church

[29] The Dinton Parish Registers are extant from 1558, but contain no
entries which throw light upon Thomas, the third son of Robert.
[30] The adjoining parish of Chilmark, disclosed some early Macy stones
in the churchyard. It will be remembered that Thomas Macy of Nantucket, who is said to have been of Chilmark, referred to Thomas Mayhew
of Martha's Vineyard as "my honored cousin" (N. Y. Col. MSS., Vol.
XXV), and while searching for Mayhew wills, I accidentally found the
will of Thomas Maycie of Chilmark, dated 1575, which may serve as the
basis of some future investigations concerning that well-known family,
whose emigrant ancestor first settled in Salisbury, Massachusetts.

and the Cathedral at Salisbury (Arch. Sarum. IV, 165), which may be taken as showing some interest or connection with that parish.

"All the evidence adduced, by inference and exclusion seems to favor the Tisbury family as the one to which Governor Mayhew belongs, and that the Tisbury branch belongs to the Dinton stock seems equally presumptive. The line of Matthew's parentage probably sprung off before the Dinton stock had their pedigree registered in 1565, and it is also fair to presume that Simon, who heads it, had more than one son. With the exception of Matthew many of the names of sons in the Tisbury and Dinton families are nearly identical, John, Thomas, Henry, Edward.[31]

"In the Mayow arms sea mews are engraved for the birds, which in the authorities quoted are given as 'birds.' It will be noticed that the arms described on the tabular pedigree have a crescent for difference, indicating their use at the time of the visitation (1565) by a second son, probably Edward, son of Robert. Thomas, the younger brother would have used the mullet for difference. The use of the mullet by Gov. Thomas Mayhew, indicating his descent from a third son of the Mayow family of Dinton, taken with the other evidence presented, leads to the belief that the Thomas who was buried at Tisbury in 1590, was father of Matthew, grandfather of Gov. Thomas, and son of Robert.[32]

"It now remains to turn to the maternal ancestry of Governor Mayhew, the Barters of Wiltshire, of whom Alice, as we have seen, married Matthew Maow in 1587. While the author[33] cannot with equal satisfaction designate beyond doubt the particular branch to which she belonged, yet the following will

[31] The Mayhews of Dinton were Roman Catholics, and according to a recent authority, had in those days suffered for their attachment to that faith. An Edward, born at Dinton, 1570, became a Benedictine monk, and with his brother Henry was admitted to the English College at Douay in 1583, and later they matriculated at the English College, Rome, 1590 (Stephen, Dict. Nat. Biog. Art. Maihew). He died in 1625. It is probable that he was the son of Henry, and was baptized at Dinton, November 12, 1571. In those days of religious ostracism and persecution, when the Puritan movement was growing in strength, it is possible that the branch to which Governor Mayhew belonged became Protestant, and thus lost association with and recognition by the parent stock.

[32] This account of the Tisbury family is condensed from an article in the *Genealogical Advertiser*, prepared by the author for that publication (Vol. IV. pp. 1–8).

[33] Banks: *History of Martha's Vineyard*, I, 112–113.

indicate her probable parentage and the tabular pedigree illustrates it:

James Barter = Margaret ....
of Fovent,
Wilts.

Edward Barter = Edith .. ..   Roger
(eldest son)   Thomas
of Fydleton,   Christian
Haxton, Wilts.

William   Joan   Alice   Christian   Edward   Ellyn   Harry   John

"The will of James Barter of Fovent, Wilts, is dated Sept. 1 1565, and in it he mentions among others his eldest son Edward and his daughter (in law) Edith, wife of Edward (Arch. Sarum, P. C. C., IV, 210).

"The will of Edward Barter, his son, of Haxton, Wilts, of the Parish of Fydleton, is dated Oct. 6, 1574, and mentions among others, his wife Edith and his daughter Alice. (Arch. Sarum, P. C. C., V, 231.)

"The will of Edith Barter, widow, of the same parish, is dated Aug. 9, 1576, and mentions among others her daughter Alice to whom she gave 'halfe an aker of wheat and half an aker of barley my best cowlett, my white pety coat, my kercher, my canvas apron a platter and porringer' (Arch. Sarum, P. C. C., V, 273).

"As this Alice was the only one found by the author in his searches among Wilshire wills, and as the name of Edward was bestowed on the third son of Matthew and Alice, presumably in honor of her father, as Thomas had been given in memory of his father, this origin of Alice Barter, the mother of Thomas Mayhew, is offered as the probable solution of the question of her ancestry.

"Of the childhood, education, and early business training of Thomas Mayhew of Tisbury, nothing definite has come to the knowledge of the author. It is presumed that he lived in Tisbury during his youth, and was educated in the parish school under the care of his parents. When his father died, he was twenty-one years of age, and it is certain that this event placed upon him the necessity of individual responsibility for

22

the future. We know that he become a merchant, but where he served his apprenticeship is unknown. Daniel Gookin, who knew him personally, says he was 'a merchant bred in England, as I take it at Southamptom.' This seaport town was, in that period, one of the most important commercial centres in as I take it at Southamptom.' This seaport town was, in that period, one of the most important commercial centres England, ranking with Bristol as secondary to the great port of London. Like all merchants of the maritime ports, he naturally became cognizant of and interested in foreign trade, and as the colonization ventures of the established mercantile companies began to develop, he must have learned of the possibilities of profitable traffic beyond seas. Among the great merchants of London, Mr. Matthew Cradock was an early adventurer in this line of business, and was among the first to support the companies engaged in the colonization of New England. In the course of business it is to be supposed that every suburban merchant in England went to London often to have dealings with the large wholesale houses in the capital, and in that way we may suppose Mayhew became known to Cradock and thus laid the foundation of their business relations in later years. In 1625, at the accession of Charles the First, Thomas[34] Mayhew was thirty-two years of age and had been engaged in business for himself in all probability for about a dozen years, since the death of his father. During that period he had married, about 1619, and family traditions and a record of some antiquity brings down to us the name of the bride of his youth as Abigail Parkus.[35] Further particularization has been given to this tradition by making her a daughter of that Parkhurst family of which George Parkhurst of Watertown, Mass., 1643, was the first New England representative. George was the son of John Parkhurst of Ipswich, England, a clothier, and his sisters, Deborah and Elizabeth, came to this country with him, and were later residents of the Vineyard, the former as wife of John Smith and the latter of Joseph Merry. So

[34] Banks: *History of Martha's Vineyard*, I, 113, 114, 115.

[35] This is from a memorandum, genealogical in its character, prepared by Deacon William Mayhew, of Edgartown, who was born in 1748, and was thus within the sphere of close personal knowledge of his immediate ancestors. He was ten years old when Experience Mayhew, the great family exponent, died (1758), and Experience was about the same age when the old governor died, thus but one life spanned the gap between Thomas Senior and Deacon William. The memorandum was preserved by the Deacon's son, Thomas, and was in existence in 1854.

23

far no documentary or recorded confirmation of his marriage
has come to light, and some considerable search has been made
to find the probable place where the marriage took place, but
without avail. The tradition is given for what it is worth.

"The fruit of this first marriage of Thomas Mayhew was a
son who was christened by the name of his father, about 1618,
and living to man's estate became the famous missionary to
our Indians on the Vineyard." No other children are known,
nor when and where the mother died. We are at present left
to conjecture as to the whereabouts of the father, as well as
his family, and not until 1628 do we find a further possible
reference to him. The Company of the Massachusetts Bay
were then actively promoting their new settlements at Salem
and vicinity, and sending supplies thither. Their records at
this time contain the following entry, showing that Thomas
Mayhew was then engaged in mercantile pursuits:

16 March 1628.

Bespoke of Mr. Maio at 10¼ p yrd for beds & boulsters 20 bed tikes.
Search likeing ⅜ broad & 2½ long & 1⅜ yrds wide: 11 yrds each bed and
boulster Mass. Col. Records, I, 35.

"In two years more Mayhew had determined to follow to
New England for the 'beds & boulsters' and 'bed tikes' he had
sold for the emigrants to the latest English colony."[37]

Thomas Mayhew the elder, of England, presumably taking
with him his wife and one son, had established his residence at
Medford, Massachusetts, as agent of Matthew Cradock. He
lived in a "greate stone house," built by his employer whose
business interests in Massachusetts were of large financial
magnitude. Edward Johnson in his "Wonder-Working Providence (1654)" thus refers in some contemporaneous poetry
to the relationship between Cradock and Mayhew:

The richest Jems and gainfull thing most Merchants wisely venter:
"   Deride not then New England men, this Corporation enter:
" Christ calls for Trade shall never fade come Cradock factors send:
"   Let Mayhew go another move, spare not thy Coyne to spend
" Such Trade advance and never chance in all their Trading yet:
"   Though some deride they lose abide, here's gaine beyond mans wit."

The author has made extensive searches in all published parish registers of English churches and similar books, for any clue to his baptism or
any reference to Thomas Mayhew. The following items are here printed,
and may be of some value Thomas Mayhowe, baptized August 20, 1617,
at St. Martin's in the Fields, London. The will of Mildred Read of
Linkenhurst, Co. Hants, widow dated August 15, 1630, mentions her nephew
" Thomas Mayhew the younger "

" Banks: History of Martha's Vineyard. I, 115, 116.

THE "GREATE STONE HOUSE," MEDFORD. BUILT FOR MATTHEW CRADDOCK,
1631, AND OCCUPIED BY THOMAS MAYHEW

Mayhew's residence continued in Medford for the ensuing five years, and during this time his personal business interests, largely investments in mills, and his duties as factor of Cradock, became hopelessly involved, more through misfortune than breach of trust. Cradock despatched a new factor in the person of John Jolliffe and the termination of Mayhew's business relations with the London merchant immediately followed. In 1637 he became a resident of Watertown, was elected a Deputy to the General Court, and appointed a local magistrate for trying small causes; he also served as selectman through the years 1638-1644, and Deputy to the General Court for the same period, thus indicating that his financial difficulties had not lessened the esteem in which he was held by his fellow townsmen.

This brings us to the time of his probable departure from Watertown to the island home where his declining years were spent. He probably removed to the Vineyard in the spring or summer of 1645—four years after their acquisition.

"When brought to New England by his father in 1631, the younger Mayhew was about ten years old, and for the dozen ensuing years intervening between that and his majority he can be pictured as attending the village schools of Medford from 1631 to 1635, and at Watertown from the time his father removed there till he had finished with the common branches taught in the primary and grammar schools. Nothing in contemporary accounts of him indicates that he was 'designed' for the profession of theology, or that he was to become a religious teacher. That this was his natural leaning appears evident from later developments, and he was given special instruction in languages, at least, after he had finished with the public schools. He was 'tutored up,' states Edward[38] Johnson, an author of that period, from which we infer not a college education, but private instructors.[39] The Rev. Thomas Prince says on this topic:

"He was a young Gentleman of liberal Education, and of such Repute for piety as well as natural and acquired Gifts having no small Degree of Knowledge in the Latin and Greek Languages and being not wholly a Stranger to the Hebrew."[40]

Banks, History of Martha's Vineyard, 1 127.
Wonder Working Providence.
[40] Indian Converts 280.

"Doubtless he found time or made the opportunity, while assisting his father, to study evenings with tutors. His usual occupation we may assume was assistant to his father in the management of the mill and farm at Watertown, and other enterprises in which the elder was engaged. The turning point in his career, however, was the purchase of this island in 1641, just after the young man had entered his majority, and his assumption, in 1642, of the charge of this venture as one of the patentees. Being thus related to the proprietorship of the soil and the management of its temporal affairs, he was the leader of the small band of his Watertown neighbors who came hither that year, and for the following four years, until the father finally came, he was the local governor of the new settlement. At this time he was still a bachelor and we have no means of knowing what were his domestic associations during that period. but when in 1646 the elder Thomas came with his family he made his home with them. With them, as we know, came the step-daughter, Jane Paine, and in the following year he made her his bride."[41]

It is to be remembered that Martha's Vineyard belonged to no chartered province as then established by royal patent excepting its relation as an integral part of the territorial grants to Sir Ferdinando Gorges. For over a score of years Mayhew never, as far as is known, made any acknowledgment of this technical relationship to the Province of Maine, and Martha's Vineyard continued to be what it was in fact—an independent, self-governing entity.

Mayhew could say with much truth:

> "I am monarch of all I survey,
> My right there is none to dispute."

This anomalous political situation was due primarily to the death of Sir Ferdinando Gorges in 1647, the governmental distractions consequent upon the Civil War in England, the usurpation of the proprietary interests of Gorges in Maine by the government of the Massachusetts Bay Colony for the following thirteen years.

.   [41] Banks: *History of Martha's Vineyard*, I, 127, 128.

27

THE DUKE OF YORK, LORD PROPRIETOR OF MARTHA'S VINEYARD

Meanwhile another factor was entering the field of colonial enterprise and management, it being none other than a scion of the royal house of Stuart—James, Duke of York, who entered into negotiations in 1663 for the purchase of the Stirling Patents. This having been accomplished, his elder brother, then Charles the Second, granted to the Duke of York on March 12, 1664–5, a Patent covering the territory of New York, Pemaquid (Maine), Lond Island "and allsoe all those severall Islands called or known by the names of Martin's Vineyard and Nantukes otherwise Nantukett." As far as known Gorges interest in these islands was not bought by the Duke of York and no attempt seems to have been made to revive it. The establishment of the Duke's government in New York resulted in the absorption of the Mayhew properties into this new and strange overlordship. Francis Lovelace, the first governor of the Duke's province, summoned Mayhew to Fort James in May, 1670, "to consult about those Parts and their settlem(en)t" and he was required to show his title to the Vineyard and "to bring all his Patents, Writings and Papers relating hereunto with him." Mayhew delayed a year before responding to these summons, probably waiting for something to turn up in political affairs which would remove this unexpected complication.

For thirty years, since 1641, he had been responsible to none, and now he was facing a crisis in his affairs at the summons of a new master set in authority over him by his "dread Sovereign Lord," Charles, the King. The conference between Governor Lovelace of New York and Thomas Mayhew of Martha's Vineyard, began July 6, 1671, and continued through the six following days, the former representing Roman Catholic royalty, and the other a product of the Protestant Reformation. The Puritan emerged from the conference with this Popish master under flying colors. He not only was commissioned as Governor of Martha's Vineyard "dureing his natural life," a royal honor conferred upon him in his eightieth year, but brought home with him the added honor of appointment as Chief Justice of the Courts of Martha's Vineyard and Nantucket, and a title hitherto unknown in the colonial annals of England—Lord of the Manor of Tisbury.

29

THE PROVINCIAL HOUSE, NEW YORK, WHERE THE CONFERENCE WAS HELD

At four score years the thoughts of the elder Mayhew had doubtless turned to the place of his birth, and the scenes of his boyhood days, as he discussed with Lovelace the favors which he wished to secure from the Duke of York. Mayhew had risen to an unique position among his colonial confreres, and the recollections of the Tisbury in "Merrie England" with its manor house and tithe barn aroused within him a desire to become the first of a line of Lords of the Manor in another and younger Tisbury in this new-found world. He recalled the Arundels of Wardour, hereditary lords of Tisbury Manor in Wiltshire, living but a short distance from his childhood home, and the grandeur of their position, holding dominion over broad green acres, with tenants filling the tithe lofts to overflowing each harvest as willing acknowledgment of their fealty in lieu of knightly service. He now wished the legitimate fruits of his own headship made distinctive and hereditary. Lovelace consented to the creation of a manorial demesne on the Puritan Vineyard under the noses of the Dissenters of Massachusetts, doubtless as an admonition that the days of Cromwell and his fanatics had passed, and that the good old customs of "Merrie England" with its county families and loyal tenantry would be restored to their wonted position.

"The following is a copy of the 'Patent or Confirmacon of Tisbury Mannor unto Mr. Thomas Mayhew & Mr. Matthew Mayhew his Grand Childe:—' "[12]

FRANCIS LOVELACE Esq: one of the Gentlemen of his Ma'ties Hon'ble Privy Chamb'r and Govrnor Gen'll under his Royall Highness JAMES Duke of Yorke and Albany &c of all his Territories in America: To all to whom these Presents shall come sendeth Greetings: WHEREAS there is a certaine Island within these his Royall Highness his Territoryes in Length over against the Maine neare East and West & being to the North West of the Island Nantuckett wch said Island was heretofore Granted unto Thomas Mayhew Sen'r & Thomas Mayhew Jun'r his Sonn by James Forret Agent to William Earle of Sterling in whom the Government then was a considerable part or Severall parcells ov wch said Island hath by the said Thomas Sen'r & Thomas Mayhew Jun'r his Son been purchased of the Indian Proprietors & due satisfaction given for the same whereof for diverse Years past they have been & still are in quiet & Lawfll Possession the Particulars of which said Parcells of Land are as hereafter is sett forth vizt That is to say a Certaine Piece of Land called Chickemote bounded on the East by a Spring called by the Name of Kutta-shimmoo on the West by a Brooke called Each-poo-qua-sitt on the North

---

[42] Banks: *History of Martha's Vineyard*, II, Annals of Chilmark, p. 18.

31

by the Sound & on the South by the bounds of Ta-kem-my: An other Parcell of Land called Keep-hickon Bounded on the East by the Westermost Bounds of Takemmy from whence it extendeth about a Mile and halfe Westward along the Sound wch is the North Bounds, and to the South reaching to the middle of the Island. Then a piece of Land called Quianaman Bounded on the East by Takemmy Pond on the West by Nashowaken.muck Pond & a foot Path wch Goeth from the said Pond to a Brooke call'd by the Name of Tyas-quin wch Brooke is its North Bounds: As also the Land called Nashowa-Kemmuck Sold to Thomas Mayhew Jun'r beginning at a Place called Wakachakoyck & goeth to the River Arkessah, running from the said Wakachakoyck by a straight Line to the middle of the Island where is the middle Line that divides the Land of Towtoe and other & the Land sold to the said Thomas Mayhew and from the Place that Line meeteth the middle Lyne soe dividing the Land as aforesaid to goe to the Harbour on the North side of the Island called Wawattick: Together with two of the Elizabeth Islands called Kataymuck & Nanrameshit & other Severall Small & Inconsiderable Islands in Monument Bay NOW for a Confirmacon unto the Said Thomas Mayhew Sen'r & Matthew Mayhew his Grand Childe the Son & Heyre of Thomas Mayhew Jun'r in their Possession & enjoymt of the Premises KNOW YE that by Vertue of the Commission and Authority unto mee given by his Royall Highness upon whom as well by the resignacon & Assignmt of the Heyres of the said Wm Earle of Sterling as also by Graunt & Patent from his Roya'l Majestye CHARLES the second: the Propriety & Government of Long Island Martins Vineyard Nantuckett & allthe Islands adjacent amongst other things is settled, I have Given and Granted & by these Presents doe hereby Give Ratify Confirme & Graunt unto the said Thomas Mayhew & Matthew Mayhew his Grand Childe their Heyres & all the aforementioned Pieces & Parcells of Land Islands & Premises to bee Erected into a Mannor & for the future to be called & knowne by the name of TYSBURY MANNOR Together with all the Lands Islands Soyles Woods Meadowes Pastures Quarrys Mines Mineralls (Royal Mines excepted) Marshes Lakes Waters Fishing Hawking Hunting & Fowling within the Bounds & Lymitts afore described And all other Profitts Commodities Emoluments & Hereditaments thereunto belonging or in any wise appertaining To bee holden according to the Customs of the Mannor of East Greenwich in the County of Kent in England in free & comon Soccase & by fealty only And the said Mannor of Tisbury shall be held Deemed reputed taken & bee an Intire Enfranchized Mannor of it-selfe & shall alwayes from time to time have hold & Enjoy like & equal Priviledge wth other Mannors witnin the Governmt & shall in noe manner or any wise bee under the Rule Order or Direction of any other place but in all Matters of Governmt shall be Ruled Ordered & Directed according to the Instructions I have already given for that Island in Generall or hereafter shall give for the Good and Welfare of the Inhabitants by the Advice of my Councell: To have and to hold the said Mannor with the Lands thereunto belonging with all & Singular the Appertenances & prmisses unto the said Thomas Mayhew & Matthew Mayhew their Heyres and Assignes to the Proper use and behoofe of the said Thomas Mayhew and Matthew Mayhew their Heyres & Assignes forever Yielding Rendring & Paying therefore Yearly & every Yeare unto his Royall Highness the Duke of Yorke his Heyres & Assignes or unto such Governor or Governors as from time to time shall bee by him Constituted & Appointed as an

Acknowledgment two Barrells of Good Merchantable Cod-Fish to be Delivered at the Bridge in this City.

Given under my Hand and Sealed with my Seale & with the Seale of the Province at Forte James in New York on the Island of Manhattans this eighth day of July in the three and twentyeth yeare of the Reigne of our Sovereigne Lord CHARLES the Second by the Grace of God of England Scotland France and Ireland King Defender of the Faith &c & in the yeare of our Lord God One Thousand six hundred seaventy & one.

"It will be thus seen that practically the whole of the present town of Chilmark with the district of Chickemmoo, now in Tisbury, and the Elizabeth Islands were erected into a Manor, like unto the ancient form known in England, and the elder Mayhew and his grandson (Matthew) were created joint Lords of the Manor of Tisbury"[43] with succession to their heirs male.

"As may be imagined, this transplanted form of manorial government with its suggestion of "lords" and tenantry and "acknowledgments" was not favorably received by the people in the adjoining towns. It gave them an insight into what would occur if the ideas were carried out to their logical sequence. But Mayhew proceeded with his plans for an exclusive domain which should be separate from all the rest of the settlements on the Vineyard. Very early he had surrounded a part of this territory with a fence, and the name of one of his divisions, Kuppi-egon, or Kupegon, meaning an artificial enclosure, is a survival of this fact. Simon Athearn gives us a commentary on the situation, which doubtless voiced the sentiments of the settlers, when he said that they 'have impropriated a Cuntery by a fenc to themselves' and again referring to the same subject in describing Chilmark: 'This included land is considered un settled but is in propr(ie)ty by a fenc made a Cross the Iland by the people of Chilmark and Chilmark is fenced by the same under their peculiar improvement,' "[44]

"In the management of the Manor granted to the Mayhews, they alienated portions of the soil, but retained the 'acknowledgment' of certain annual, or more frequent, payment of trifles to signify their manorial privileges. During the lifetime of the elder Mayhew none of the manor was alienated, except two pieces in the Quansoo region, to his grandsons John and Thomas Mayhew, and it is not known that he demanded any quit-rents from them. In a sale of a part of the Elizabeth

[43] Banks: *History of Martha's Vineyard*, II, Annals of Chilmark, p. 20.
[44] Banks: *History of Martha's Vineyard*, II, Annals of Chilmark, p. 22 3.

Islands, however, he instituted the custom of requiring quit-rents, and the first case was that of John Haynes, who agreed to pay "2 good sheep at the Manor House on November 15th yearly and every year."[45] It is not known where the 'Manor House' was, if it existed in anything more than name. Possibly it was the house occupied by John Mayhew at Quansoo, or Quanames. After his death, Matthew Mayhew, as surviving patentee, kept to the custom of requiring the annual payments of such 'acknowledgments' in true English style. Usually in the mother country the quit-rent was 'a good fat capon,' to be delivered at Christmas or Whitsuntide, or oftener, but Mayhew varied his requirements to all sorts of small articles. One was obliged to bring annually to him 'a good chees;'[46] another 'one nutmegg' as a tribute,[47] and he required 'his beloved brother John,' who was permitted to occupy certain land, 'one mink skin' to be paid yearly 'at my mannor house in the mannor of Tisbury,' on the 15th of November each year.[48] Benjamin Skiffe was made to bring 'six peckes of good wheat,' annually.[49] As late as 1732, Sarah, widow of Thomas Mayhew (3), in a deed to her two daughters conveying land in Chilmark, referred to the 'Quitt-rents which shall hereafter become due unto the Lord of the Manner . . . . which is one Lamb.'[50]

Opposition to this grafting of manorial privileges and dignities on the simple life of the Vineyard farmers extended to the point of rebellion, led by Simon Athearn, with a dozen or more who thought with him that New England was no place for such an institution, and saw no need of a governor holding position for life. They demanded his abdication of this office and refused acknowledgment of his lordship. Arrests, fines and imprisonments followed and for a while turmoil ensued, but with the Charter of Massachusetts Bay, dated October 7, 1691, providing for the jurisdiction of that colony over the present territory of Massachusetts "together with the Isles of Capawick and Nantuckett near Cape Cod," the source of power and influence of the Mayhews waned, and the days of their life tenures and manorial privileges ended.

[45] Duke- Deeds, I, 45.
[46] Ibid., I, 346.
[47] Ibid., I, 265.
[48] Ibid., I, 27.
[49] Ibid., I. 118.
[50] Ibid., VI, 56; Banks: History of Martha's Vineyard, II. Annals of Chilmark, p. 21-22.

IONATHAN MAYHEW, D·D·PASTOR OF THE WEST CHVRCH
IN BOSTON, IN NEW ENGLAND, AN ASSERTOR OF THE CIVIL
AND RELIGIOVS LIBERTIES OF HIS COVNTRY AND MANKIND,
WHO, OVERPLIED BY PVBLIC ENERGIES, DIED OF A NERVOVS FEVER,
IVLY VIIII, MDCCLXVI, AGED XXXXV

GREAT GREAT GRANDSON OF THOMAS MAYHEW

"The transendent genius of his day who threw all the weight of his great fame
into the scale of his Country."

(John Adams)

"He was the father of civil and religious liberty in Massachusetts and New
England."

(Robert Treat Paine)

The Mayhews engaged in a contest against this transfer of their allegiance in which they were abetted by the New York authorities but it was a losing fight. Tenants continued to pay their nutmegs, cheeses, mink-skins, lambs and wheat as quit-rents for a generation, more as a means of retaining their titles than as acknowledgment of manorial rights. The grand dreams of the Wiltshire yeoman to re-establish in New England the social precedence of his branch of the armigerous Mayhews of Old England, begun under the most favorable of royal auspices, led a hectic existence, and gradually became an object of ridicule in the next century. In the Vineyard records reservations in title were made with respect to persons pretending to exercise manorial rights but it is not known how long these pretensions were effectively enforced. They are not referred to after 1756 when the Proprietors of Tisbury recorded their protest against this continuance in the following language: "Whereas sundry Persons have of late years Presumed to sett themselves up Lord Proprietors of Land in sd Tisbury in Defiance & Contempt of said Pattent and thereby caused great Disturbance in sd Town both to the Church and state and Expense of much money & Pretious Time," the townsmen voted to consider and address the Governor and Council of New York regarding the persons who were "the Cheefe Carryers on of the Disturbance."

Notwithstanding these continued rebuffs it is believed that the later line of the Mayhews continued to preserve this pleasant fiction of their manorial rights up to the time of the Revolution, when all existing claims to social caste went into the discard, with the signing of the Declaration of Independence.

The line of male descent of this family is now represented, as hereditary lord, by Mr. George Pickering Mayhew of Hartford, Connecticut.

Note. All the illustrations of this monograph are published by permission of the author of *Martha's Vineyard*.

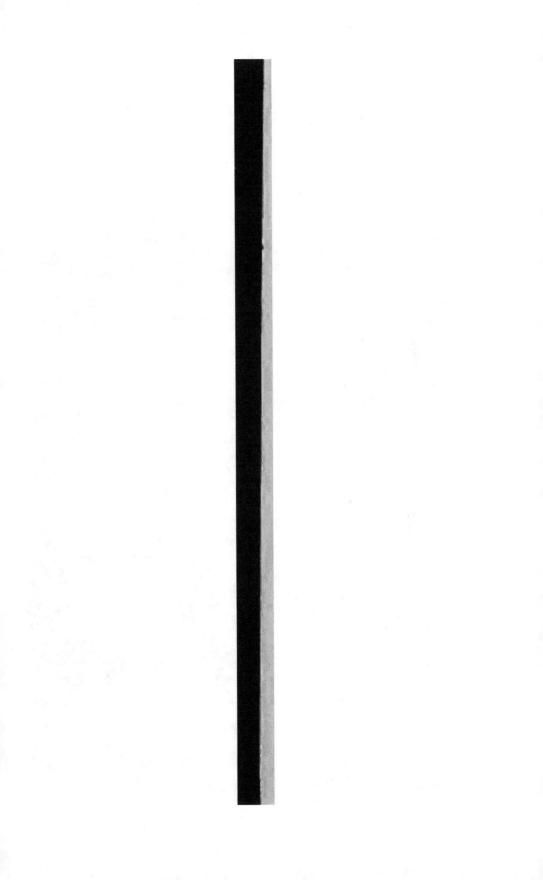